MYRIAD OF
A SOUL

SYDNEY GALLAGHER

MYRIAD OF
A SOUL

BELLE ISLE BOOKS
www.belleislebooks.com

ISBN: 978-1-958754-44-3
Library of Congress Control Number: 2023902103

Designed by Sami Langston
Project managed by Robert Pruett

Printed in the United States of America

Published by
Belle Isle Books (an imprint of Brandylane Publishers, Inc.)
5 S. 1st Street
Richmond, Virginia 23219

BELLE ISLE BOOKS
www.belleislebooks.com

belleislebooks.com | brandylanepublishers.com

For my brothers, Jose, Andrew, Tyler, and Mitchell, who were there for me at my worst.
For my sister-in-law, Liza, who supports me as a sister better than I could ask,
and for Cameron, who's watching down and is the source of so many poems.

TABLE OF CONTENTS

ACKNOWLEDGEMENTS

First, I'd like to thank my mother for investing so much of her time to help me through the sleepless nights of editing and panicking over whether I would be a successful author or not. I'd also like to thank my editor and designer for creating the most perfect version of my debut book that I could ever imagine. Thanks to my project manager, who answered every question with patience and kindness, and for keeping me on schedule for this project while I lived a hectic life as a high school student. And finally, thanks to my father and brothers, not only because they'd be annoyed if I did not include them in my acknowledgements, but also for being so protective and vowing to help me market Myriad so that I would not have to worry about anyone buying this book. Thank you all!!!

MEADOWS

The soft petals of tickling flowers are scattered
    throughout the field,
Covering almost every inch of which my bare feet do
    not stand
Alone.
Like pillars of support.
A bubbling crystal dancer weaves its trickling way
    through,
Breaking the flowers' domination of the land and
    quenching their thirst, the savior that they have
    been longing for, the benevolent breaching of earth.
A tree weeps.
Her name is Willow.
She stands alone in the middle, sagging from the weight
    of time.

I long to run to her, to take her hand and ask,
"Why do you cry? You are not alone, for you have me."
And so, the Weeping Willow replies to me.

"Surrender to the feeling of being alone, it is refreshing
    when you accept it.
"Surrender to the knowledge that I am not alone, that
    my company is not like me.
"Surrender to the inevitability of time, let it touch you
    but not wear you.
"But truly, you must surrender to the certainty that your
    brothers and sisters are killing me and my friends.
"I do not blame you, for it was not you, but it was you,
    and it was me, and we are surrendering to be your
    slaves of progression."

And just like that, upon the crying tree's words, the
    meadows, the beautiful meadows, start to

d
  i
     s
       a
         p
           p
             e
               a
                 r

LEAVE

I am encompassed by the girl who hates me and the girl
    who does not know me
        Everywhere I go, they soar after me like vultures
Scavenging for a weakness to attack
                                Why?
How?
                         How do they not see?
The absolute best way to hurt me is to befriend me?
              I am completely and utterly alone.
It nags and burns, this loneliness.
                       Always there.
Always reminding me.
                  Always whispering,
No one is here for me.
               No one wants to see me.
No one is talking to me.
                    It is my fault.
I've been hurt.

                   I've been broken.

The best way to hurt me is to

                Befriend me then…

        Leave.

Sunrise, Sunset

Sunrise in colors of pink and gold,
Sunrise, the start of stories told.
It's beautiful, the sunrise,
People stop their cries
And look at the origins of old.

Sunset in colors of orange and red,
Sunset, the end of dread.
It's beautiful, the sunset,
Listen to the cry of the alouette
And look at the end of stories old.

Between the rise and set of the sun
People fearfully run.
They hide and laugh and smile
And all the while
They're waiting for the shot of the race gun.

Sunrise in colors of pink and gold,
Sunrise, the start of stories told.
Sunset in colors of orange and red,
Sunset, the end of dread.
Sunrise, sunset, sunrise, sunset
Listen to the cry of the alouette.

DEAR YOUNGER ME AGAIN

Dear Younger Me again,
Remember when the world was about to end?
We kept on smiling, we kept on swimming
Searching the sights, the sunlight dimming.

But when we thought the world was going to
    end, it did not
And the look of beauty was forever imprinted
Because when the world was about to end,
And the nurses started to tend,
It was just a story
And in the remix, it was me.

So, keep reading your books
And don't care about your looks
Because I'll be back
And we'll listen to the soundtrack.

The world's not going to end
Because I'm writing
Dear Younger Me again.

WHAT IT MEANS TO ME

Long nights mean nothing to me,
Long days are an epitome.

Long nights have comfort:
Blanketed and snuggled in my bed
A good book in my hand,
Picking at the quilt thread.

Long days are exhausting:
I smile and laugh
But I'm in the rapids,
Searching for a raft.

I think I see a raft, but no, it's sunset
And I smile, antsy for the comfort of my bed.

Long days are an epitome,
Long nights mean everything to me.

DANCE

Look at me, I'm dancing!
I'm weaving and laughing and spinning
Pirouette, plié, sauté de Basque
Smiling, I am not lost.

Look at me, I'm dancing!
    I have so many things to say
But I don't have the time of day.

Look at me, I'm dancing!
I am here and alive and well
No one is looking—but, oh well.

Just look at me, I'm dancing!
Am I accepted into your world yet?
Almost, almost, don't you fret
I'm almost accepted in your world
And now you see me whirl,

So, look at me, I'm dancing!

MY LITTLE PRINCESS

I see the illusion of a four-year-old you, wearing a
    purple Rapunzel gown.
She's smiling oh-so-wide, but now you wear a
    broken crown.
Tell me why you cry
'Cause I can see the hurt behind your smile.

Why do you wear a tear-stained dress, my little
    princess?
Don't you know how beautiful you are?
I don't know what you're going through, but I
    promise to be there for you.
Keep your head up, my little queen,
For a moment, just listen to me.

One day, I promise, your angel eyes
Will look in a mirror and see a real smile.
It might take a while, my little child,
But I'll be there for you every step of the way.
I won't walk away.

BYE-BYE, DRAGONFLY

Bye-bye, dragonfly
How does it look, from the sky?
Bye-bye, dragonfly
I'll miss you as each day passes by.
Bye-bye, dragonfly
Fly, fly, fly, take your time.
My sweet dragonfly,
        I'll see you on the other side.

Welcome to the Future

Welcome to the future
There's so much to see
Robots, flying people, and green policies.

Welcome to the past
It feels so empty
Cobblestone, corsets, and ships crossing the
sea.

Welcome to the present
There's a lot going on
Voices, anxiety, and earthly decay.

Welcome to the future
    I wonder what it will be like
Welcome to the past
    I wonder what it was like
Welcome to the present
    I wonder what it is like.

LEADERSHIP

Leadership is a word often misused.
It's told like a benevolent dictatorship, but never
    admitted to.
Dictatorship is control,
Leadership is teaching.
Leadership is subtle, a presence in the room,
It's not sweeping what you don't like away with a
    broom.

Leadership is opening the door for someone you
    don't know,
It's striking a conversation when you see they're
    alone,
It's smiling at strangers you pass in the street,
It's inviting someone to your lunch table when
    they have no one to meet.

Leadership is taking charge and being fair.
Being a leader does not make you a powerful heir.
You can be a leader, yet never in charge
It's so simple, yet people check into Power's
    lodge..
And so, I try to teach
But I'm not going to preach.

Leadership is being yourself
When no one else
Knows who to be.

APOLOGIES

This is me with no apologies.
You can beg and beg but you will get no "I'm
    sorrys."
This is me with no apologies.
I didn't ask if you didn't want to see.

Yes, I dance, yes, I write, and yes, I sing.
I'm opinionated and my honesty can sometimes
    sting.
I am special enough to be living now.
I'm not yet at my final bow.

This is me with no apologies.
You can beg and beg but you will get no "I'm
    sorrys."
This is me with no apologies,
I'm like no other starfish in this sea.

Shine the spotlight on me,
It's time for you to see
What I'm really like behind the pleasantries.
I am not what I was like in seventh grade,
I've grown and matured, and I've got a lot to say.

This is me with no apologies.
You can beg and beg but you will get no "I'm
    sorrys."
This is me with no apologies,
Ready or not, the spotlight's on me.

MYRIAD

Myriad, by definition, means ten thousand,
An indefinitely great number of things.
I possess a myriad of dreams,
A myriad of hopes and wishes
That people will never know.

The only person inside my mind is me,
The only spirit in my body is mine,
And yet I seem to have enough dreams
For everyone in the world to take one from a
    magician's hat.

If I could have that black silk hat
And pull a dream from it every day
And it would come true
Where would I be?
Where would everyone be?

I suppose, on deeper thought, I could alter some
    dreams.
I could make my fear disappear, and not its
    physicality,
I could make it so I could be who others wish I
    was.

I possess a myriad of dreams
But I keep changing them to fit everyone else's
    needs.

ROBOT

Sometimes I feel like a robot,
Programed to go through the motions,
Programmed for one set of tasks.

But I want to do other things
Lift the glass to the lips - Control Panel.

I want to explore
Walk to class and smile - Control Panel.

I wonder what it's like to be a bird, flying
    wherever I please whenever I please
Information on the dove loading…

I ask so many questions
Most commonly asked Google question loading…

But Control Panel never has the answers
Open textbook to page 394 - Control Panel.

I should throw away my Control Panel
Information on the Cold War loading…

I should not be at the mercy of others
Go to locker - Control Panel.

No. I will not be your robot.
Resetting bot #7001235 in
3 . . .
2 . . .
1 . . .

Hello? Bot #7001235 is ready to comply.

Middle of the Night

The middle of the night is a strange place.
It's dark, full of life and suspense.
The middle of the night is a strange place
Because in the middle of the night, I often
    dream.

I dream of travel,
Far off lands where dances are new, and food is
    fresh.
Oh, the dances would be so fun to learn,
Immersing myself in the center of the
    beginning of every culture,
Then dining with my instructors on the food
    they grew in their backyard.

But what about a place where the sun sets at my
    feet,
And I can grab the sun without getting burned?
Colors blending together in an elegant mural
    where everything becomes a silhouette
And then once it gets dark again, I can lift the
    sun back into the sky,
Begin a new day and a new sunset.

And then I would visit countries on the edge of
    the world
Where I could sail to the stars,
Talk with them and tell them my stories they've
    watched from afar.
And then I could take some of their dust and
    shine, their wisdom and knowledge home
    with me.

I could sprinkle the heavens on every soul I
    met.
I could put a little hope from above in the
    troubled hearts of humans I know.

Yes, the middle of the night is a strange place,
But what is the night
Without a dream?

DEAR BULLIES

Dear Bullies,

Yes, I know you know me.
Yes, I know you've never heard my voice.
But I have a few things to say
So, hear me out?

I'm sorry for whatever I did
I didn't mean to.

I don't strive for discord and pain
I only wish for peace.

I'm sorry that you need to hurt me,
But I promise to take your unwitting verbal
    abuse
So no one else
Needs to feel what I do.

But I think you might want to stop
Because I've learned how to deal with pain
And I don't think you have.
Do you want my help?
Do you want my words of wisdom?

Yours truly,
Your voiceless victims
And (hopefully) your friend

INSIGHT

Insight,
Seeing in me,
I think I have insight.
All my thoughts, I simply create.

I think of what has happened—
Travel, loss, and laughs.
I think of what will happen—
Repercussions, titles, and graphs.

But what about what won't happen?
I don't know, I just think.
What if what isn't happening
Is because of me?

Insight is a strange word.
It's a strange concept.
I just hope to gain it one day.

For now,
I'll just pray.

MOMENTS

Everything happens in a moment.

Life starts in a moment:
The screaming child takes their first breath,
The next moment they are ushered away by a
    doctor,
The umbilical cord connecting to their mother
    is cut in a moment.

Isn't it strange to think about moments?
Jobs start in a moment.
A call says, "You're hired!"
But they can end in a moment too.
A boss hollers, "You're fired!"

It only takes a moment for someone to lose
    their mind,
Go crazy and pull the trigger,
In a moment they become a murderer.
In a moment someone's heart stops beating,
And in a moment their loved ones start
    screaming.

But there are the better moments.

The moment when you step off a plane in a
    new place,
The moment when you get into your dream
    college,
The moment when you have your first kiss,
The moment when you say "I love you" for
    the first time,

The moment when you're hugging your
        parents cause you're about to move out,
The moment when you get married and have
        your first child.

Another new life

Life starts in a moment:
Your screaming child takes their first breath,
The next moment they are ushered away by a
        doctor,
The umbilical cord connecting to their mother
        is cut in a moment.

And as you look at your child you marvel
        at how you were once that small and
        dependent and innocent.

It felt like just a moment ago.
And you realize,

Life is just one moment.

Wings

A bird without wings is flightless.
A boat without a sail is stationary,
Flightless and stationary, but not useless.

A bird without wings is beautiful.
Pastels thrown onto feathers,
A comforting pink and baby blue blend softly
    together.
How snowflakes blend into a slope
One indiscernible from another
But creating a breathtaking sight each time.

A boat without a sail is a home.
Housing a family while they sleep,
Housing from the cold rain pounding above their
    heads;
Keeping them warm through the night.

I may not have my wings.
I may not have my sail,
But I am warmly housing a pastel bird
A pastel bird who is growing her wings.

MIRRORS LOOK BETTER

"Mirrors look better,"
My brother said
What that means:
"Mirrors portray me,
I am happy,
I am me,"
So his reflection
Is finally free.
He doesn't care
What people say,
Because he's Tyler
Because he's at liberty
"Mirrors look better"
My brother said
Said to me.

Salty Rain

The natural rain made of salt and water
    cascades,
A waterfall of emotion raw and unfiltered.
The scientific solution with which you clean
    yourself,
White turned red from the feelings bursting at
    your seams.

The red turns to water
And so you begin the purgery of pain.
The innate ability to lose sense of who you
    want to be
And become what you need to be in that
    moment.

All life begins with this weightlifter.
Your parents hold you and love you
Talk to you and care for you.

And you repeat history
Loved, held, and cared for.
It is so easy to forget
Just how miraculous tears are.

INVISIBLE

It's not always bad being invisible—
You get to hear everything people say without
    them knowing you heard.
Think about it:
    A mirror is invisible.
And I am, at my core, a mirror.

I reflect what I see and what happens to me:
My brother accidentally elbows me, I elbow
    him back,
My cousin bakes me a cake, I give her cookies.
I display Greek sunsets, Italian bakeries,
    Croatian oceans I once visited,
As well as the panic attacks and harassment
    from my stranger peers.

Invisibility isn't always bad.
Yes, it hurts sometimes,
I'm not ashamed to admit it.
But everyone loves a good mirror, even if
    they forget about the cracks on the edges.

EYES

You can't see it,
But I see how you break behind the mirror.
You smile and laugh and act like everything's
     alright,
Then you pass by a car window and see your
     reflection
And your face drops like Niagara Falls

It's just for a moment.
If I blinked, I would've missed it.
Sometimes, I think I'm imagining your lack
     of self-confidence
But then, I remember you told me you cried
     last night
Because you had a mirror in your room.

Just know that I'm here for you,
Because I'm not blind
If you would just open your sparkling eyes.

Space Between

There is a little space
Between each breath.
The world stops rotating for a moment
And resets itself.
You rebalance,
You redo,
And start speaking.
Your oxygen renews.

Oxygen and breathing are different.
Breathing is taking in air just to keep going
Oxygen is not taking in gas so you can sing.
It's the connection between your mind and
    body,
The system at which you don't lose your
    sanity.
Open your mind and you will see
That oxygen only comes when you know
"Someone loves me."

And so with the oxygen renewed
And as the world and your heart meet,
I will see you
In the space between.

WIZARD OF OZ

Hey, Wizard
Wizard of Oz
Can I have some help? I've heard of your
    cause and I'm
Tired of feeling insignificant.
Can I be your client?
I'll be blatant, been feeling a little distant
I probably sound absurd…

Hey, Wizard?
I'm balanced on the edge of a knife,
About to fall off, but to which side of my life?

Hey, Wizard
Wizard of Oz
Don't walk away yet, just take a pause.
What's wrong with the tin man?
Will you give me his armor and take my
    broken heart?
And how about the scarecrow?
I'd give anything to have a quiet mind—you
    can give him mine
And the cowardly lion…
We have some stuff in common.

Please don't tell me it's darkest before the
    dawn
Because it's pretty hard being withdrawn.

Hey, Wizard
Wizard of Oz

I've talked and talked but your lips are still
     drawn.
If you're really the Wizard,
The Wizard of Oz
Why do you do nothing to help my cause?
Because if my mind is Dorothy,
(I'm not in Kansas anymore, Toto)
Change me to the unbroken tin man.

Hey, Wizard of Oz
Are you walking away without a second
     pause?
I'm talking to myself, sounding completely
     absurd,
Help me calm this blizzard.

GLUE

There was a girl who I once knew.
She laughed and loved and was the glue.
She tried so hard, she had to fight.
She fought so hard just to survive.

She needed to be remembered by the greats.
Her greatest wish, but she felt locked in a crate.
She pushed to be remembered until her last day.
I feel so bad; she still had so much to say

She smiled at me like everything was fine,
But I knew that she was still lost in her mind.
It's strange to think that all this time
Her thoughts were bitter like fresh lime.

I panicked when my glue started to unstick.
I scrambled and scrambled to hold in the bricks.
I still remember clearly the day that she died.
All I could think was "My glue has dried."

She has gone onto another life.
She laughs and loves, and I hope she's alright.
Sometimes, I do admit—
Sometimes, I still wish…

I wish for my glue to come back.
I wish for my life to stop being pricked by a
    thumbtack.
I wish I could still see my glue.
I wish I could see the girl I once knew.

Because there was a girl who I once knew.
She laughed and loved and was *my* glue.
She tried so hard, she had to fight.
I fought so hard to help her survive.

SNOW

Falling
Falling
Falling

Dancing
Dancing
Dancing

Crystalized
Ice
Plummets,
Lies down
And sleeps
On my eyelashes.

It shivers and curls up in a ball,
So small, so innocent,
It's strange to think
That this petite little snowflake
And all her family
Can drown me.

But still she dances
And still she falls
And now she's kind.
She just wants a break.

She sleeps on my eyelashes,
Her mother on my nose,
Her brother in my hair,
Her sister in my hand,

And her father drifts onto the
unforgiving ground.

Crystalized ice
You can go ahead now
And sleep.

SHAPES

"Don't try to fit the square peg in the circle."
I am not a square, or a circle, or a star:
I am not any of the shapes that have pegs in this
    wooden, rigid society.
My shape is ever-evolving, too inconsistent to stay.
Here I sit, in the shadows of their happiness,
Of their easy fit.
I don't know, I'm a dreamer:
I hope and I wish and I start—
I wish there were another wooden board,
One I could sit in.
No borders, no walls,
Shapes shifting and blending and thriving together.
I beg for shapes to not exist.
But the bitter truth is that they do.
I accept that truth, let it torture me as it does.
"Don't try to fit the square peg in the circle."
I am not a square, or a circle,
Or any of the shapes born perfectly in their mold.
I wish they would listen when I say that shapes
    should be irrelevant,
But I'm hidden silently in the shadows of my
    dreams.

CLOUD

I find it interesting
How we call the Internet "The Cloud"
Like it's a white fluffy mystery and we are toddlers,
We try to find shapes and discover the sky's secrets.
Is technology really the sky below us?
Instead of craning our necks up to see a beauty of
    wonders, we slink our eyesight down to watch the
    horror stories of our existence.
This cloud is like the serpent of the great sky above.
It lays coiled under the table, its dangers known but
    often ignored.
When it gets sick of being ignored, it strikes the ankle
    of one of the people sitting at its shelter.
Cacophonous fear silently drives everyone to stand on
    top of the table.
The snake is all people can talk about for days before
    they precariously sit down again
And when the serpent shapes into a messenger of
    good for a day, no one notices.
No one stops staring at portraits of the serpent to
    appreciate the joy,
The Cloud really is a mystery.
There are secrets and stories untold littering its sky
    like plastic tends to the sea.
We should call it "The Dragon."
It breathes fire on those who speak too loudly for the
    wrong reasons,
But offers refuge and a ride on its back to those who
    deserve it.
We cower in our huts that are mostly flameproof,
Losing all color to our skin as we stare into the blue
    light that reigns us in.

I'm not saying that the dragon is all evil.
It is good, but like all, has its cons.
I'm just saying it's untrustworthy and cunning,
The reptile ready to strike,
And that we should all be wary of her battle plans.

ONE TYPE

This place, this place,
This crazy place.
It was built for one type of person.
The smart person,
The funny person,
The popular person,
The athletic person,
All put into one.
Here, it is filled with hundreds, thousands, of
    that person.
They get along and laugh along,
They all blend
Into one person
And it confuses me.
I mix up names,
I mix up faces,
I mix up personalities,
Even though they are all the same.
I am not the person that this place was built for
And I don't have the voice to speak out about it
I keep quiet just so I don't stand out.
They know I am not the person to fit in here.
But they don't talk about it,
If ignorance is bliss, then I am anguished as hell.
I know all the differences and I am not ignorant
    to them,
I don't care about them.
But they do.

But I won't complain.
I won't talk about it.

Because this place has its benefits,
A blessing hidden far beneath the center of the
     core of its curse.
I reach through the curse in the empty points to
     grab hold of the blessing.
I cradle it close to my chest and to my heart and
     I weep into her pillow,
And then I wake up,
And I come back to this place,
And smile along like I belong,
Even though we all know I don't.

MAMA

"Mama" is possibly the best word to ever be invented.
It brings satisfaction to my lips to hear it fall off my
   tongue.
"Mama" is the word of Grace,
Of love and respect.

Grace is her name, but only secondly.
My first knowing of her was Mama.
Most people know her as Grace,
But Mama fits her better.
She claims we are her five most important people
So what better way to call her than Mama?
Simplicity speaks louder than eloquence.

Love is in the contract, but it's my choice to follow.
How could I not love my mom?
She's intelligent and quirky.
She dances gracefully through life as if it were a stage.
She's the Snow Queen in our production of the
   Nutcracker
She is even more of a queen than Elizabeth II.

She defied death five times in choosing to be a Mama.
She cried in the darkness of pain just to see our faces,
Then after that pain and the blandness of the hospital
   room,
She put up with us being children.
She deserves a prize for all that.

In our Nutcracker family, we all have our roles.
Dad the Snow King,

My biggest brother, the soldier,
My big sister, the princess,
My other big brother, Fritz,
Me, the sheep
My little brother, the dragon.
But it's not the Nutcracker without the beautiful
    Snow Queen.

HEAVEN'S ANGEL

I'm trembling,
And I doubt it's from this room's cold.
I am shaking now,
And I doubt it's from the tremble's hold.
I reach out and take your hand,
And I smile as you pull me around.

Let me see you in all your glory.
Heaven's angel doth back fall on Earth.
    Let me fly on the back of your wings,
Soar over the golden gates that lead to you:
An oasis glowing bright and when the match
    loses its light,
Heaven's angel shall fall back to Earth,
The Cosmos light burning with mirth.

I HAVE...

I have been in pain before
I have seen the dark quench the light of hope
I have gone through the motions, no matter
    the chore
I have been through endless nights where I
    could not remember to cope.

I have seen a starless sky
I have walked the road where maps have not
    traveled
I have endured the venom of a snake bite
I have felt the strings of my soul begin to
    unravel.

I have been beaten and bloodied
I have been broken and hurt
I have gone through the world, lonely
I have been held too close to the fire to remain
    unburnt.

I have been hurt in many ways
I have felt the icy bite of unforgiving running
    air
I have sat calmly through the mindless blaze
But I never changed when they asked
And it was for the better

KNOWLEDGE

All I know right now is that I don't know.
I don't know what I wish for.
I don't know what I dream about.
I do know that I want things to get better,
But I don't know how I know it.
I don't know how it could get better at the
　　moment.
I lie in a sunny paradise filled to the brim
　　with sand and saltwater.
My anonymity is assured.
I don't know about my anonymity
Though, it helps me escape the dangers of
　　everyday reality,
I don't know if I want it
Questions roam my mind as an orange leaf
　　drifts in an autumn breeze.
I don't know the answers to any of them.
I guess I have lived enough to know that no
　　one ever really knows anything.
It's all a game where we change along the
　　way until the end.
Do any of us truly win?
In school we are given knowledge then tested
　　on it,
But in life we are given tests then receive
　　knowledge.
How do we know if we pass or fail?
Take the word of one person?
How does that person decide?
How do we know that person ruled our case
　　justly?

So now I can safely say, while being shielded
    from the truth,
Never knowing if it's good or bad,
That all I know,
Right now,
Is that I don't know.

DEAR RIVER HOUSE

Dear River House,

Hi, it's Sydney again.
Remember me?
When I was only the tiniest of infants, I first
    graced your crumbling walls.
My family tore down walls,
Broke down buildings,
Painted and crafted,
Until you became the high-maintenance
    masterpiece you are now.
The memories I have in your waters and yard
    are the best I will ever have.
Sleeping on the boat overnight,
Napping in the hammock,
Trying to climb the tree, then realizing that
    it's too big and high,
Swinging over the burning fire pit,
Jumping on and off the bunker;
All these precious memories haven't included
    everyone else yet.
What about staying out till two in the
    morning talking with my family?
What about the island where we swam out to
    find a shark's tooth?
And running outside, dirt becoming the
    permanent marker on my shirt and legs?
What about my bare feet pounding the grass
    and sand as I throw myself onto the
    tube, the smile of purest joy straining my
    face?

Pushing everyone off the tube and taking a
    break to play King of the Hill?
Sunset cruises on the boat?
Dance parties in the middle of the night?
Testing our limits on the golf carts?
Becoming siblings with my cousins?
No one will ever understand your beauty
Or the way it works when we take your
    shelter.
The dynamic between us here is not
    something we can explain
Chaotic and messy are the biggest
    understatements that can be made,
But it's an anxiety-free and happy zone.
It's the heaven that when I die, my soul will
    fly to and take eternal rest.
Please, please, please, river house, don't you
    ever change.
It would break me to see heaven crumble.

More Love Than I Can Say,
The infant that broke you down so she could
    build you up again.

Long Live...

I vividly remember
The sword's clash was the sound of the
    thunder,
The rose you gave me lay bleeding on the
    ground.
I could hear every scream, each sound as the
    rose lay dying,
The sword's clash was the sound of the
    thunder,
And through the rumble and rubble, I still
    heard you say,

"Save yourself.
Think of everyone else.
That rose was gone anyway,
Don't let its memories waste your life away.
When they look into your eyes,
Don't you want them to see the beauty of a
    starry night sky?
Walk away from this battle,
Don't lead yourself to the slaughter with the
    cattle.
Grow from this memory,
And don't let it inhibit you from being free.
And when they tell your story, let them say all
    night and day…
'Long live the princess
Who ran from the castle just to save her best
    friend.
Long live the princess
Who fought off a dragon just to make a
    friendship.

By her example all the girls who don't want to
	be a damsel in distress,
They now know how to save themselves.'"

And so from the battle, I sorrowfully walked
	away.
The guilt of abandonment held me captive,
	even when I would pray.
You called me a princess, but what angel would
	I be,
If I cannot reign over that battle victoriously?
It was years, years, years ago,
But I'm stuck in that loop and all I hear is a
	murder of crows
Circling, circling, circling over me.
I'm stuck there, losing control over my court,
	wishing things were how they used to be.
Isn't it strange
How trauma and change
Shape us forever?
No matter how much we hate it, the past is
	cleverly forever.

Too Beautiful, Darling

TBD:

An acronym used by teachers everywhere
    when deciding project due dates.

"To be determined."

The test date is "to be determined."

When you'll know your grade is "to be
    determined."

I have grown to hate TBD.

I have learned to hate writing those letters
    together.

Everything I've ever associated with those
    letters has been anxiety.

Those letters have become stress and late
    nights of cramming,

But when did they become such a negative
    aspect of my life?

They are just letters.

I can change them.

I can change their meaning.

How about something uplifting?

Something sweet and drizzled with honey?

Something like… "too beautiful, darling."

That sunset is "too beautiful, darling."

Your painting is "too beautiful, darling."

That's just "too beautiful, darling."

But I suppose, if I thought about it,

You are TBD.

You are to be determined; you do not know
    who you are,

You are too beautiful, darling.

In every sense, you are TBD.
But aren't we all, just a little bit,
TBD?

ALL ALONG

Please don't take this wrong, I'm still doing
     well
No new nails have broken my shell
I'm still stuck at home.
I still read my books when I'm feeling alone.

But something doesn't feel right without you
     here.
I really wish that I had you near
I miss you
And I wish I could see you,
But there's use for hopeful wishing.
Are you listening?

I'll write a letter in a bottle and toss it in the
     sea,
A special message for you just from me.
I hope it finds you wherever you may be.
I sent a boat out across the ocean.
The cargo is my clunky emotions.
I want you to feel my devotion,
I look up at the stars and hope you're looking
     at the same ones as me.
I can't wait till the sun sets, knowing it's you
     I'll see
How could things go wrong?
Cause you've been here for me all along.

WE ARE YOUR FUTURE

Times are changing
So fast and so sudden the past can't keep up.
They scan the analysis of words from
    others,
Searching for guidance and answers
What they don't understand is…
We are your answers.
We are your futures; we can give you the
    answers.
Still they silence us with words of
    condemnation:
"You haven't lived long enough to know."
"You're so young, what do you know?"
    I know that I am your legacy,
I know that I am the force that will carry
    your memory and your world into the
    next era.
Yes, the past is wise.
Yes, we will take your advice and learn from
    your mistakes.
Walk into the sunshine and relax,
Let the future make their own mistakes.
And from the rubble of repercussions,
Let us use what you learned to create the
    next utopia.
We are young, but that is the point.
We carry the world on our shoulders in
    silence
While ideas meant for you explode wars
    inside of our bodies.
We're aggressive because we have to be

If the past keeps shutting us down with the
    stories of their wrongs,
There is no hope for the future.

You have had your time on the stage,
But everything has changed since you lived
    your stories.
It's our time in the spotlight.
You want to be remembered, so you are
    reluctant to let go of the attention,
Outlandish acts desperate to keep things
    how they were twenty years ago.
If we don't take the stage now it'll be an
    endless cycle of silence and destruction.
We are your future.
Let us take charge.
Let us tell you how it should be and lead
    you to the next realm of the times.
Rather than let the past continue to rain the
    ruins of their society on what we are
    building.
"You're so young, what do you know?"
I know that we are your future.

GOD SAVE THE OUTCAST

God save the outcast who's living just outside,
Who's looking through the window, wishing she
    were warm inside.
God save the outcast who's waiting patiently to
    be welcomed,
Who's peeking in, waiting to be seen.
If the outsider is getting on fine,
Why would angels pay any mind?
Past words must be revised
And change them to one worthy of other eyes.

God bless every outcast of present, future, and
    past,
Bless them with the power to walk through the
    door
And start up a conversation without feeling the
    chore.
Mary, raise the outcasts.
Let them feel like a son or daughter of God,
Especially when their hearts throb.
Gabriel, visit the outcasts,
Tell them of their destiny,
Lead them to it carefully.
Angels, guard the outcast,
Love them and protect them,
Teach them to march to the beat of their own
    drum.
Cherubs, play with the outcasts,
Let them know they are part of Heaven's great
    plan.
Show them they are imagining the feeling of

being stepped on like ants
And most of all,
The largest request:
God, bless the outcasts.
They are your children and need your love
To fit in, they don't need to fit the glove.
God, please, bless the outcasts
We need your guidance,
We don't see the shine of our own diamonds.
God bless the outcast.
Do not underestimate us.

Running Wild

Something's always broken.
The house, the pier, the boat, the ramp.
Everything's always dirty.
Sand stuck between my toes,
Dirt under my nails,
Mud smeared across my cheekbones and jeans.
But the wind will run wild once a month
I'll laugh and let my hair fly and tangle in the
    dance Mother Nature taught it.
When it rains, I'll steal away to dance in the dead
    of night,
Heaven's tears soaking me through.
When the wind is tired,
And the rain is playing with another place,
I'll stay out with the angels,
Talk with them,
Tease with them,
Laugh with them,
Terrorize the grass with them,
Clean the soap off me with dirt and sand and
    grass with them.
I'll stay out with them till the sun nears
    consciousness,
And then I'll be dragged back to the crumbling
    bricks and age-old blankets
And prepare to do it all again tomorrow.
With the sun out, we do it all again.
We push each other, bathing each other in the
    holy water.
We ride the waves, laughing when we fall,
Boards and boats and tubes turn into flying

Pegasi,
A cloud of sand and ancient relics is the
    homeland.
Far from the shore, but we've known how to
    spread our wings since birth.
We live side by side.
We take only the most trusted of non-angels.
I might let you come see this beautiful place,
But only if I can see you in my life forever.
This place is my home.
If heaven were a place,
If heaven dropped onto Earth,
It would be here.
These sacred grounds are graced only by the
    blessed,
And the blessed are always running wild.

Un-Woman

"You know, you really should eat less."

"No one likes the fat girl."

"Oh my god, you're a skeleton!"

"Would it really hurt you to eat a burger?"

"You like STEM? Nerd!"

"You don't throw yourself into school? Airhead."

"You look anorexic, girl, go eat some carbs."

"Stop eating carbs, they'll make you fat!"

"Don't wear heels, you're too tall already."

"Put on some heels, no one can see you down there!"

"Guys can't concentrate, put on clothes!"

"Leave it all to the imagination."

"Show some skin and be proud of your body."

"I can see your bra strap."

"Don't starve yourself."

"You need to lose weight."

"Boys will be boys."

"Better seen and not heard."

"Is that a form-fitting dress? You look like a whore."

"Do you even have a body under all those baggy clothes?"

"You don't need money or a personality, guys will do it all for you."

"Be individual! Don't let a guy be a human for you!"

"Why don't you have a boyfriend? Are you a lesbian?"

"This is your fifth boyfriend? Slut!"

"Stop being such a bitch."

"Are you on your period?"

"Calm down!"

"You're too young."

"You're too old."

"Raise your voice, let society hear you!"

"Stay quiet, no one wants to listen to you!"

"Women run the world!"

"Stay down, girls, this is a problem for the guys."

"Are you seriously cooking? You're so 1950s!"

"You can't even make me *dinner*? What kind of woman are you?"

"You're not a *real* woman."

"Why are you sad? You have no reason."

OVER HER SHOULDER

Her friend left,
She walks alone.
Her keys are jammed between her knuckles,
Her stance is tense,
Her shoulders are tight as she glances over
    them for the seventh time.
Make that eight.

A whistle sounds from the other side of the
    street.
"Hey, baby, what's the matter?"
"Why are you so tense?"
"Come over here, baby."
"Let us buy you a drink."
"Relax a little."
"C'mon baby, let's have some fun."

She ignores them and keeps walking,
Glancing over her shoulder at the drunks who
    were yelling at her, and
Two of them have brass knuckles.

She hurries her walk, pulling her jacket tighter
    around her torso,
Shivering despite the warm air.
Her mind whirs with anxiety as she turns her
    head from over her shoulder to her outfit.
Skinny jeans, boots, a t-shirt, and a leather
    jacket—
Was it her outfit that was causing the
    unwanted attention?
Was it her French braids?

She glances over her shoulder for the eleventh
   time as she enters the parking garage.
Were those men calling out to her or to the
   woman across the lot?
Finally, she makes it to the safety of her car,
Jams the keys in the ignition, and sighs in
   relief, laying her head on the wheel.
It is over,
The night is over.
Safety is guaranteed,
At least until the next night, but tonight,
She just cries softly alone in her room, unable
   to complain since she doesn't have it the
   worst.
But at least she won't have to look over her
   shoulder anymore tonight.

Too Young

According to society, Gen Z is too young
Too young to use our voices
Too young to have an opinion
Too young to make a change
Too young to know anything
And yes, you are right
I am too young
I am too young to be scared for my Black
    friend's lives
I am too young to have supremacy
I am too young to be scared to walk alone at
    night
I am too young to feel his eyes trailing me
I am too young to be raised in a world where I
    expect violence
I am too young to be desensitized to the words
    "school shooting"
I am too young to have to put a new "Justice
    For…" every other day on my Instagram
    story
I am too young to fear my friends going to
    conversion therapy
I am too young to have to worry about police
    brutality
I am too young to have to listen to an orange
    President who uses pedophilia to his
    advantage
I am too young to have to worry about being
    shamed for my body
I am too young to have to apologize for being a
    victim

I am too young to have to know how to use my
    whiteness to stop a racist scene
I am too young to have to convince everyone
    else that Black lives matter
I am too young to be tired of prejudice
I am too young to live in a violent, polarized
    world where everything is political
I am too young to fight for the rights over my
    own body
I am too young to need to place other people's
    health over mine

I am TOO YOUNG for racism

I am TOO YOUNG for sexism

I am TOO YOUNG for transphobia

I am TOO YOUNG for homophobia

I am TOO YOUNG for constant death

I'm too young…

WORDS

My words get tangled up in my mouth.
They trip and fight and then fall out.
If only I could retrace my steps somehow,
Things would look clearer now.

My words always come out wrong,
They come out a moment too long.
If only there was a way to right all the
    wrongs,
Things would flow like a song.

My words don't always come out right,
It feels like I poured some darkness into
    light.
If only they would hear between the lines,
Things would sound alright.

My words trip and fall the wrong way,
But listen, my speaking is when the words
    start to decay
Read my writing, your mind might start to
    sway
'Cause things would sound the right kind of
    way.

BLACK AND WHITE

When you see everything as black and white,
Are you sure that you won't mind?
    Are you ready to see me
In all my undignified glory?

Cause I fit in the gray
And everything starts to fade away.
I don't fit inside the lines.
I've been told I am wrong a couple thousand times.
Society messes with my head.
I open a magazine, and my insides feel dead.

I could never be the pretty little princess
In a pretty little dress,
Seemingly effortless.

I could never be one of those beautiful people,
I could never look that regal,

And you know I can easily say,
I am effortlessly gray.

ANGELS

Been spreading my wings since day one,
And I've decided that I've won.
It's a fickle game, this life,
I know I won't live it in strife.

You don't know what you live for until it's
        gone.
I'm preparing to start moving on.
You don't have to live for anything,
You just have to live for everything

I know this is not the end.
I've only decided to make friends
With the saints in the sky.
When I cross the finish line,
All I need is for them to be on my side.
I need them to be mine.

I can see heaven in the long run
And I know
It's coming home.

You can go ahead and crown me at the gate.
I've lived my entire life in wait
I've been adventurous so I would know
I had a spot among the angels.

Hey, Society

I'm sorry I'm not your dream girl
I'm sorry I don't rock your world
I'm sorry I don't live up to your fantasies
I'm sorry I'm not what you think you need
    me to be.

I'm sorry I'm not what you made up in your
    imagination
I'm sorry I don't comply to your unrealistic
    expectations
I'm sorry that in this world, I feel no respect
I'm sorry that you see me as incorrect.

I'm sorry that I have to apologize
I'm sorry you think I don't qualify
I'm sorry you don't appreciate me.

Hey, Society?

I'm actually not all that sorry.

Princess Barbie

I hate that I dream of being Princess Barbie,
Beautiful, charismatic girl.
Everyone loved her.
She never had to work for her Prince Charming.
He fell in love with her, things were alright,
Happily ever after, after just one fight.

Thanks to Princess Barbie, I thought I'd be
    Queen by now.
I thought my life would be all planned out.
I thought the bad guy would always lose
And the good guys would never light a fuse.
I thought the antagonist would be clear as day
But even the protagonists have some things to
    say.

I hate that I break because I'm not Princess
    Barbie.
I don't have a Prince Charming yet because I
    don't have a flat tummy,
But what if I don't want my Prince Charming
    yet?
    And what if my best friend wants a princess
    instead?
What would Princess Barbie have said?

DEAR MR. STYLES

Dear Mr. Harry Styles,
Thank you.

Thank you for your music.
It lifts me with angel wings to the high heavens,
It keeps anxiety at bay on long nights,
It keeps the thoughts light when the day is dark.

Thank you for your voice.
The calming aurora of its sunrise keeps me
        grounded,
Its soft crescendo lifts my heart—
There's no other way to describe it.

A video of you comes up on my Instagram feed,
And I can't help but smile
Playful, serious, laughter, and everything in
        between
Make me feel less alone.
But most of all,

Thank you for being my best friend in my head
When the world turned its back on me.
I'm just a little girl with big dreams,
Just like everyone
And like no one at all at the same time.

Thank you,
Thank you, Mr. Styles.

Best,
The little girl with big dreams

LETTER TO MY LOVE

In the evening, under the stars,
The night so black,
So velvety soft,
Am I just a temple of wounds, my love?
The future burns brightly,
My flesh is cut,
The blood is sharp as a knife as it draws patterns
    across my skin.
Nothing but stars and night,
A blanket against the cold,
My cold, cold blood that makes my dress,
My dress that twirls in the moonlight as I dance
Barefoot on the hot, liquid ground,
Splattering my bare legs.
Will you wake me from this dream, my love?
This beautiful, wonderful dream?
Is this all just a dream, my love?
All of everything is but a dream
Oh, my love, my love,
Please don't wake me.
Let me dance under the starlight once more.
The black night is so velvety soft
The floor is made of liquid, and it supports me
As I float.
It's warm, it envelops me,
My love, won't you come feel this floor?
Won't you wrap yourself in the blanket of the
    night sky?
Come wear a dress of blood with me, my love.
Don't fear the falling, it's just part of the dream.
We fall and we fly,

Our wings made of our cut up flesh,
This is such a beautiful dream, my love
Come join me in this abyss.

And under the evening stars,
The night so black,
So velvety soft,
I wear a dress of my blood.
My body is a temple to wounds, my love.
Come join me in the abyss, my love.

SLIM-THICK

Hip bridges, wall sits, forty-five minutes of core,
Three workouts a day just to get what society asks
    for.
Make your waist thinner.
Make your booty thicker.
Allow the wiggle but lose the arm jiggle.
If you have cellulite, hide it away from sight.
Acne is forbidden, your stars are uncalled for.
That should be it, but they ask for more.
Have your belly be flat,
Lose every ounce of back fat.
A dimple on your cheek but not on your back.
A symmetrical face with a smooth jawline.
Thick thighs but still have a gap.
Round, perky breasts and a sharp posture,
Slender fingers to munch on snacks that never
    seem to linger.
Melodious voice and a soft laugh.
Short enough to make him feel tall
But tall enough to reach the top shelf.
Tiger stripes aren't allowed.
Order a salad but don't eat it.
Be athletic but never better than him.
Have their children but never hold the baby
    weight.
Never make anyone wait.
Long hair, no makeup, but still look like Gigi
    Hadid.
How can I ever complete this impossible deed?
Be 5'7" and 5'2" at the same time.
I'm not that magical, and I'm losing this rhyme.

Hide your hip dips,
Have full lips,
Bright eyes and glowing skin,
 Never do any sins.
 If I wear a crop top, I'm called a slut.
 If I wear baggy clothes, they call me a slug.
 If I have this body, I'm making little girls feel
  bad.
 If I don't have this body, I make everyone else
  feel sad.
 Be happy all the time.
 Get straight A's.
 Don't be a nerd.
 Don't be a dork.
 But don't be the popular girl.
 Have lots of friends.
 Don't have too many boyfriends.
 Don't have an ego that's too big.
 Most importantly, be slim-thick.

HELP.

it's 10:00 at night.
i've barely made a dent in my homework
i've been working on it since 7:00.

jumping off my roof and breaking my legs
    sounds appealing.
that way, i don't have to turn in any assignments
that i will inevitably be working on until 6:00 in
    the morning.
i would just get to lie in the hospital bed
do nothing,
sleep,
curl up around a book,
cuddle my stuffed hedwig,
sebastian stan,
anthony Mackie,
tom holland,
all 5 members of one direction
sitting around me,
being my besties.

i've been crying over my history assignment for
    the past twenty minutes,
the same assignment i've been working on for
    three hours
and still need to write 700 more words.
i don't know what's on my chemistry quiz
    tomorrow
let alone what we had on our test last week.
i'm already behind enough in English,
lord of the flies makes me even more depressed.

i don't understand a lick of Spanish.
no sé, señora.
i don't have enough brain cells for math,
i thought a log was part of a tree.
i haven't gotten a good night's sleep in at least
    two and a half months.
the sports requirement just gives me more
    anxiety.
i haven't spent real time with my friends since
    before winter break
and it turns may on saturday.
when i do sleep, it's nightmares.
my only coping mechanism is creating a false
    reality in my head.
my therapist thinks i'm fine because i don't talk
    to her.
i depend on coffee to walk around and smile.

so, i don't see how jumping off the roof
and breaking my legs
is a bad idea

Our Definitions

If I could choose my last words, it would be these:
"The most interesting trauma filled with the most
　　beautiful people."
What a heartbreaking ideology, and yet…
I still love it.
It's so strange how our definitions turn us and twist us
　　into humanity.
I guess that's all humanity is,
The clashing and crumbling and combining of our
　　definitions,
"The most interesting trauma filled with the most
　　beautiful people."
My trauma pushed me from the ugly people
And all the beautiful people I've met, I've grown into
　　and out of and loved forever.
I wonder what would happen to humanity if we all left
　　our definitions in the kitchen
And walked hand-in-hand up the mountain.
I wonder what would happen if we brought our
　　definitions with us, too.
That's all history is:
　　The misunderstanding of our definitions.
How many lives would be saved if we dropped our
　　egos and talked to each other about our definitions.
My brother put it best, the world is
"The most interesting trauma filled with the most
　　beautiful people."
　　What a heartbreaking, perfect sentiment.
But that's what all of our definitions are.

ABOUT THE AUTHOR

Sydney Gallagher is a high school student in Telluride, Colorado. She is the fourth of five children, values family above all else, and is a lazy perfectionist when it comes to her schoolwork. When she was eight years old, she lost her sister Cameron due to sudden cardiac arrest at the 2014 Shamrock Half Marathon. She advocates for teen mental health through her family's foundation, the Cameron K. Gallagher Foundation. Sydney has a morbid obsession with true crime, fantasy novels, and romance novels, all of which keep her awake well past midnight.

CPSIA information can be obtained
at www.ICGtesting.com
Printed in the USA
BVHW041942270423
663177BV00002B/78

9 781958 754443